I was Broken, Too

I WAS BROKEN, TOO

Four Paths to Restore Hope

Barbara Higby

ELM HILL

A Division of
HarperCollins Christian Publishing

www.elmhillbooks.com

I was Broken, Too

Four Paths to Restore Hope

Published in Nashville, Tennessee, by Elm Hill, an imprint of Thomas Nelson. Elm Hill and Thomas Nelson are registered trademarks of HarperCollins Christian Publishing, Inc.

Elm Hill titles may be purchased in bulk for educational, business, fund-raising, or sales promotional use. For information, please e-mail SpecialMarkets@ ThomasNelson.com.

Library of Congress Cataloging-in-Publication Data

Library of Congress Control Number: 2019932501

ISBN 978-0-310107552 (Paperback)
ISBN 978-0-310107569 (Hardbound)
ISBN 978-0-310107576 (eBook)

This book is dedicated to the One who restores hope,
to the broken whose hope is battered,
and to my husband who walked with me on these paths to hope.

CHAPTER 1

Who Doesn't Want a Miracle?

"Nana, you're pretty nice for an old person." The ice cream scoop in my hand froze mid-air and I slowly turned to lock eyes with the nine-year-old. I didn't speak but my expression must have said volumes because Noah immediately began to backtrack.

Pacing, hands fidgeting, he tried again, "It's not that you're *old*. It's just that you're—you know—you're in between adult... and elderly."

I handed him the bowl. "Eat your ice cream, Noah."

This is the same grandson who told me why he loves coming to Nana and PopPop's house: "It's like the Garden of Eden—with marshmallows!"

I may have marshmallows, but as an adult who has endured much (and is not yet elderly) I can assure you that I live in no Garden of Eden. The losses I've suffered would not be found in that sinless paradise and I'm sure the pain you have endured would not be there either.

If we sat together and shared stories, our specific circumstances would differ but we would find our struggle for hope to be the same. Disappointment, offense, and pain have marched into our lives—uninvited invaders. They vandalized our joy and devastated our hope. At times they crept in softly, but often they blatantly barged their way in. However they entered, they broke through our protective doors and wreaked havoc. The despair that accompanied them caused hope to falter and eventually fade, leaving us to wonder if we will ever recover.

Fading hope is like fading light—it darkens our surroundings. We don't choose to go to this dark place, but neither do we choose to not go. Life's assaults weaken us and, in our diminished state, they carry us to places where fear threatens and vision dims. In the midst of the darkness we can't see a way out and the prominence of our problems obscures the hand of God. It's a shadowy, murky place to live. I believe this is where the widow of Zarephath lived when Elijah found her.[1]

At one time, love flooded her heart and her infant son's smile all but overwhelmed her. There were no bounds to the happiness she and her husband shared. Indeed, they felt honored to be blessed with a son. As they watched their child grow, each stage of development thrilled them with fresh wonder.

Her maternal heart beat with unquenchable joy, until the day it didn't. Until the day her husband left her a widow. Until she found herself poor and defenseless. Until famine ravaged the land and she watched her precious son waste away. Until she had nothing but a handful of wheat and a little oil. Her joy was long gone by then. Hope had vanished. She shuddered at what she saw in her future—death by starvation for her and her son.

Perhaps that's why, when the prophet came to town and asked her for a cake, she prepared it for him, using the flour and oil that was intended for her and her son's last meal. What difference did one meal make when there was no hope for a next meal? Had she given up? Or, did she feel a reverence for the prophet's God? Did the God she likely did not know instruct her heart to respond? During the preparation of that final meal, did the widow feel hope flicker?

She alone had been approached by Elijah. When he saw her gathering sticks for a fire, she was the one he asked for bread and water. She weakly explained that she didn't have any bread and the sticks she was gathering were to cook a final meal for her and her son. Elijah's next words must have sounded absurd. He said, "Don't be afraid." Don't be afraid of starvation? Don't be afraid for tomorrow? Don't be afraid of death? Lurking fear had usurped her hope, as it does ours, and the prophet exposed it with his simple statement.

Elijah continued, "Go home and do as you have said. But first make a small cake of bread for me from what you have and bring it to me, and then make something for yourself and your son." Did he know how irrational that sounded? If she first made a cake for him, there would be nothing left to make another. But she did not have time to puzzle over the impossibility of his request because Elijah was still speaking.

He said, "For this is what the Lord, the God of Israel, says: 'The jar of flour will not be used up and the jug of oil will not run dry until the day the Lord gives rain on the land.'"

We do not know if her obedience was out of resignation or hope, we only know that she did as Elijah told her. I would love to read her thoughts. Could she have believed what he said? Was there reason to hope? There was nothing to lose when she was already one meal away from starvation. But she didn't starve. Miraculously, there was food every day—for her, for her son and for Elijah. The jar of flour was not used up and the jug of oil did not run dry.

You and I understand personal famine. We have experienced decimated joy and shriveling hope. Who of us wouldn't want to experience a miracle of that magnitude in the midst of our desperation?

Perhaps you, too, became a widow who was left to raise a family alone. Or you became a single parent through the pain of betrayal. Maybe you suffer the unnatural sequence of a parent outliving her child. Did your resources, like the widow's, dry up and leave you unable to supply your own needs? It could be that you've been abandoned by a child, parent, spouse, or friend. Is poor health robbing you of ability, energy, a future? You may find yourself without employment, without healthcare, without direction. Have you experienced one loss after another until your hope has been depleted?

This book offers to restore your hope. I cannot assure you that your loved one will reconcile or that you will get a new and better job. I cannot promise improved health or finances. I cannot erase your pain or restore your loss. But I can offer you four paths that will renew your hope.

Notice that in the story of the widow's miracle, Elijah did not simply appear and fill her jars with flour and oil. He required her to do something. It had to take an incredible amount of strength and resolve for her to press forward.

It will require the same of you when you choose to step onto the paths that lead to hope because hope has many enemies. Among them are weariness from the battle, incapacitating fear, and the inability to dream. Is it possible to envision a future through the debris of personal devastation? Yes.

- We can look through the lens of pain and find meaning.
- We can recover from the loss of one we deeply love.

- We can feel significance when all that defined us crumbles.
- We can trust again after being deserted.

There may be no motivation to test these paths other than, "What have I got to lose?" but stop and answer that question. What *do* you have to lose? The path of hopelessness is a downward spiral that will continue to deplete your spirit. I know. I lived there—the place where you may now live. The place of brokenness.

It is a place where depression threatens, lethargy holds us captive, and fear hovers everywhere. But the terror of being swallowed by the darkness can prove beneficial, if our desperation shakes us to attention and incites us to fight. The threat of being consumed can rouse in us a desperate hope for rescue and push us forward for one more battle. This critical juncture will determine hope's revival or demise. Although I was broken, thankfully, I chose to fight. I followed four paths that renewed my hope, found in the anagram, H-O-P-E.

These paths are H—Hold your Eyes Higher, O—Open your Heart, P—Ponder the Positive, and E—Expect Grace. But before we explore them, let me tell you my story.

---

[1]   1 Kings 17:7-16

For Personal Reflection

Points to Ponder

- Fading hope is like fading light; it darkens our surroundings. We don't choose to go to this dark place, but neither do we choose to not go.
- You and I understand personal famine. We have experienced decimated joy and shriveling hope. Who of us wouldn't want to experience a miracle of that magnitude in the midst of our desperation?
- It had to take an incredible amount of strength and resolve for the widow to press forward—it will require the same of you.
- Hope has many enemies. Among them are weariness from the battle, incapacitating fear, and the inability to dream.

Thoughts to Journal

- Identify the uninvited invaders who have pushed their way into your life.
- Think about your personal famine. What are your needs today?
- Elijah asked the widow to participate, to act. Consider what God could be asking of you in your current situation. Don't think too big, just identify one step—maybe it's simply finishing this book.
- Describe your place of brokenness. Name everything you have lost.
- List the four paths of H-O-P-E.

CHAPTER 2

Forever Changed

Alexander Pope wrote, "Hope springs eternal in the human breast." I would contend that there are times when hope doesn't *spring* forth. Sometimes it barely trickles. Nevertheless, it is there. A trace of hope can usually be found somewhere in the human heart, even when buried under rubble. I say that because I had a heap of wreckage pressing down on my hope. Debris already littered my life from unpleasant church issues and hurtful accusations, but that was nothing compared to what was to come. I would soon be blindsided by pain that threatened to smother me.

It was one of those days when the brightness of the blue sky lifts one's heart and lightens the weight of a busy agenda. My husband and I had off that Monday and were ready to enjoy the sun-filled October morning by eating breakfast out before picking up our daughter, Stacey. She had one of her debilitating migraines and it was arranged that we would bring her and her three-year-old daughter to our house. Although a mother herself, Stacey needed some TLC from her mom.

As we prepared to leave, the phone rang—it was our son, Corey, and his voice sounded uncharacteristically serious.

Corey and his wife, Shannon, lived downstairs from Stacey and her husband, Phil, in a two-family house they bought together. Stacey and Shannon worked on opposite days and conveniently watched each other's child while the other worked. This morning Corey called to tell me that Stacey had been taken to the hospital and urged us to get there quickly. I noted his urgency but felt no alarm because Stacey had been hospitalized before for her migraines. As we drove to the hospital, I mentally listed the friends I would call for prayer once we learned Stacey's condition. Sun streamed in the car windows, belying the emotional climate change that would soon assault us. Upon later reflection, Corey's phone call sounded ominous, but on that bright Monday morning I had no suspicions. Neither did I know that, as awful as this day would prove to be, over the next few years one lifetime dream after another would crash and burn, leaving me in ashes.

When we gave the desk attendant Stacey's name, my husband saw him visibly react, but I was oblivious. I was still making plans to bring her home. I couldn't wait to see my daughter. From infancy she was an emotional power pack with high highs and low lows. I was anxious to reassure her and calm her concerns.

We were led to a small room where Stacey's husband was waiting, along with a doctor, social worker and nurse—far too small a space for so many people and the gravity of the news that was about to be shared. I was impatient. I just wanted to see Stacey. Although the doctor spoke slowly, I could not comprehend his words. I wondered why all these people were there and why this was taking so long. I thought, "Just tell us what's wrong and let us see her."

Even as I recall it now, I can feel the slowness of my comprehension, like a whisper tiptoeing into my mind. Surely they couldn't be saying what I seemed to be hearing. Dumbfounded by the emerging realization, tears and words spilled together. "You don't mean... she's dead!" In an instant, the weight of the room, Phil's demeanor, the crowd of people and their somber countenances told me it was true.

"Please," frantically I begged one and then the other, "Go back. Look once more. She might be breathing. Please, just check one more time!"

But they didn't go back and look. They knew. It wasn't until I took her cold hand in mine that the truth became real and then I knew, too. Stacey had died.

Pain seared my heart; it seemed beyond human endurance. There was no relief, no remedy, no cure. The pain could not be understood, rationalized or explained. Stunned, I wondered that I could endure such intense grief and still live. How was I breathing?

We planned her funeral against the backdrop of a threatening church implosion. Her memorial service would take place in the church that had been the joy of our life, but was now filled with hurtful suspicions and increasing division. Within a year, the friends who brought us comfort in our bereavement, believed accusations about us and ignored our pleas to talk.

In addition to losing our daughter, in three years' time, we also lost our church, my husband's pastoral position, cherished lifelong dreams, and dear friends. Hope? It was dwindling fast and I knew that if I didn't recover it, I wouldn't survive.

Under the weight of sorrow upon sorrow, amazingly, somewhere deep within, hope still flickered. Haltingly, I made choices that set me on a course that would restore my hope. This book tells of my journey and the four paths I walked to find hope again. I share them as a weary traveler who was dangerously close to losing her grip. My struggle, sad to say, is not uncommon. If you are in the place of faltering hope, let me assure you that the paths that led me back to hope promise to bring you there as well. Read on and find hope, whatever your challenges may be.

For Personal Reflection

Points to Ponder

- Sometimes hope barely trickles, but a trace of hope can usually be found somewhere in the human heart.
- The pain could not be understood, rationalized or explained. Stunned, I wondered that I could endure such intense grief and still live. How was I breathing?
- Hope? It was dwindling fast and I knew that if I didn't recover it, I wouldn't survive.

Thoughts to Journal

- What has forever changed your life?
- Are you able to accept that there is blessing hidden in the rubble?
- Look for the flicker of hope that still resides in your heart and trust that it will ignite as you read on.

_____
_____
_____
_____
_____
_____
_____
_____
_____
_____
_____
_____
_____
_____
_____
_____
_____
_____
_____
_____
_____
_____
_____
_____
_____

H

CHAPTER 3

The "H" Path

We were grammar school kids walking home from school, chattering about those things young girls find important when, *thwonk!* Regina walked straight into a telephone pole, head first. When the stun wore off we asked, none too gently, "What in the world were you doing?" Regina often tripped and, apparently, on this day she was literally applying her mother's advice to watch where she was going. While concentrating on her feet, careful of every step, Regina neglected to look up at the bigger picture.

We walk through life a lot like Regina. When tripped up by difficulties, we try harder and concentrate on every step and misstep. Though we avoid a rock and step over the cracks, we lose sight of where we're headed and crash along the way. Nursing a headache, we turn even more introspective and increasingly focus on our worries and woes, which are many and varied.

Rising like telephone poles that block our path, we are hit with a scary diagnosis, rebellious child, or job insecurity. Troubles clamor for our attention and drain our energy. The search for a way out of our difficulties or a path around them exhausts us.

Once the stun subsides, fear contends for our attention and presses in. Worries abound and we fixate on the *what ifs*. What if I can't make my next payment? What if I never marry or have children? What if I don't get this job? What if I do get this job? What if the rumors are true? Preoccupation with worry makes hope elusive at best. How can hope survive when our attention zeroes in on our problems? Could a change of focus renew our hope?

It can and does, when we apply the H of hope—Hold your eyes higher.

Keep your Eye on the Bell

Nine-year-old Zoe surprised me when she said she wanted to attempt the rock-climbing wall. I watched her harness up, admiring my granddaughter's adventurous spirit. Once secure, she started the climb but didn't get far when she began to struggle. Flailing, she finally pushed off and eased the rope to let herself down. Her face wore defeat and her lower lip quivered as she listed all the reasons she didn't make it to the top. The footings were uneven, the wall grazed her knee, she got confused where to step next and which rock to grasp. We stood back and watched others nimbly climb the wall and ring the bell at the top, proclaiming their success. I knew Zoe would try again.

This time she scaled the wall easily and grinned down at me when the bell rang out her victory. Once her feet were back on the ground, I asked her why she succeeded this time. "I didn't look at the footings at all and I shook it off when I hit the wall," Zoe said. Then she added the zinger, "I just kept looking up at the bell." Zoe learned a lesson that day that extended beyond rock-climbing.

When We Can't See the Next Step

When we lose our footing in life we become distracted. We can't find a foothold or figure out which way will lead to the top. We hit the wall, our bruises smart, and hope wavers, leaving us with a choice—do we accept defeat or do we change our focus and keep going? The H of hope offers us a toehold that boosts us from the dark valley to an elevated plain. The H of hope challenges us to hold our eyes higher. This calls for a conscious decision to divert our attention from present problems and lift our eyes above the circumstances.

When my friend discovered a lump in her breast, Janis instinctively inventoried her family's cancer history. Realizing the potential seriousness, she asked friends to pray and found a doctor with a good reputation. The trust she placed in her oncologist was not disappointed and after minimal treatment the doctor's initial report brought good news. The threat lifted and hope flourished. But the respite was tenuous and negative news soon followed.

Janis learned that the tenacious cancer had recurred. The tumor now penetrated deep within the pectoral muscle and her doctor advised chemotherapy to shrink the invader and thereby pull it out of the muscle. Surgery was certain but first chemo was recommended, hoping that its success would make the surgery less invasive and promise a better outcome.

Fear came knocking and Janis hoped what any of us would hope—that the chemo's side effects would be minimal, that it would dissolve the tumors, that the doctor would deem radical surgery unnecessary. Thankfully, Janis had a steadfast faith because the chemo did make her ill, the likelihood of a mastectomy loomed large, and the doctor strongly recommended surgery. Janis relied on the truth of Psalm 60:11

(MSG): "Give us help for the hard task; human help is worthless." She lifted her eyes above her physical circumstances and looked to God.

Janis faced the chemo, weakness, sickness, and hair loss with peace. She underwent surgery, therapy and more chemo with grace. Through disappointment, sickness, and pain, Janis was valiantly carried because she did not succumb to what she saw with her eyes. She steadfastly focused higher, on the Savior who is mighty to save—and He did, giving her joy and supernatural peace through the difficult journey, exactly what He's always done when His children look to Him.

Isaiah's Offer of Hope

God's chosen people needed the H of hope and Isaiah knew it. The Israelites were in Babylon against their will, enslaved to those who didn't know or honor God. The first verse of Psalm 137 tells us that they reacted as we do when we are overwhelmed, "By the rivers of Babylon we sat and wept when we remembered Zion." They wept with longing—for home, for a normal life, for a way out. And they complained.

Didn't God see their plight? Didn't He care about their pain? How could a God who chose them to be His people and professed to love them leave them in bondage? He was all-powerful—He rescued their forefathers from Egyptian slavery and parted the Red Sea! Where was He now?

Isaiah answered the Israelites' quandary with a series of questions. "Do you not know? Have you not heard? Has it not been told you from the beginning? Have you not understood since the earth was founded? He [God] sits enthroned above the circle of the earth."[2]

In effect he was saying, "You're looking for God's presence—apparently you've forgotten that He is here and has been since the earth came into being." Then Isaiah offered them the H of hope: "Lift up your eyes on high."

> Lift your eyes and look to the heavens:
> Who created all these?
> He who brings out the starry host one by one,
> and calls them each by name.
> Because of his great power and mighty strength,
> not one of them is missing.[3]

Isaiah directed their eyes to the Creator, a reminder that the God who knows the stars by name knows the predicament of His people. The same great power and mighty strength that keeps track of the stars, keeps track of their lives.

Today Isaiah's words also remind us that Creator God, the Sovereign Lord and Almighty King, knows what He is doing. "The Lord is the everlasting God, the Creator of the ends of the earth. He will not grow tired or weary, and his understanding no one can fathom."[4] He understands what we do not understand and has plans that we cannot imagine.

Unfathomable Understanding

"As the heavens are higher than the earth, so are my ways higher than your ways and my thoughts than your thoughts."[5] Isaiah again points us to a higher place. A place where God's plans are beyond understanding, but not beyond fulfillment. Our resources fall short and our strategies crumble, but God is not limited.

When we look above our earthbound line of vision, it's important to maintain our focus and keep our eyes from flitting back and forth. When despondency threatens and we are uncertain of our future, we need to stop and ask ourselves Isaiah's questions. "Do you not know? Have you not heard? Has it not been told you from the beginning? Have you not understood since the earth was founded? He [God] sits enthroned above the circle of the earth."[6] Yes, Isaiah, we know God is there. It's just that we forget because our eyes aren't fixed upward. We're looking down again.

Hold your eyes higher—higher than the earth you walk on, higher than the troubles that pull you down, higher than the mire of bills or dread of disease.

The God who names the stars will not forget us. He created us in His image to rule the world and reflect His glory. The Lord of the universe has engraved us on the palms of His hands[7] and is mindful of every detail of our lives, even when those details seem clouded to us.

Clouds and Sunshine

On days when cloud cover hides the sun I can feel chilly and a bit blue—but the sun still shines. Its presence and function does not depend on whether or not I see it. Clouds do not affect the sun's existence, only my mood and perspective.

The answer to fading hope is not found in solved problems but in changed focus. God is on His throne, even when my understanding is clouded. In a powerful, active realm, higher than the world we see, One is ruling who knows every rock, root, and danger in our present path. He knows how long the trail is, how steep, how rocky, how narrow. He knows every turn in the road and where resting places and refreshing streams are found. God is attentive to our walk and holds our hand when we face obstacles. He is not too weak or tired to intervene. More than that, He has a purpose for that path and knows where it leads. He alone sees the end from the beginning. And He does all things well, always.

Rather than groping for a change in circumstances, let's focus on the all mighty, ever loving, always faithful, utterly sovereign, all-wise, "Is-anything-too-hard-for-the-Lord?" God. Unlike human help and earthly solutions, God is the Deliverer who never disappoints. He always comes through, strengthening, guiding and upholding us.[8] He instructs and teaches us, counsels and watches over us.[9] He works all things together—the good, the bad, the ugly—for our blessing, and He makes good on His promises, every time.[10]

Hope revives when we move our focus from our problems to the God who loves us. We defeat despair when we restrain our emotions and remove them from their lead position. Our step lightens when we steadfastly maintain there is sun behind the clouds.

Hold your eyes higher than your earthbound problems and look at the One who is above it all. You will find hope—it worked for me and it will work for you.

2   Isaiah 40:21-22
3   Isaiah 40:26 (NKJV)
4   Isaiah 40:28
5   Isaiah 55:9
6   Isaiah 40:22

7   Isaiah 49:16
8   Isaiah 41:10
9   Psalm 32:8
10 Romans 8:28

For Personal Reflection

Points to Ponder

- Fear contends for our attention and presses in. As worries abound we fixate on *what ifs.*
- The H of hope offers us a toehold that boosts us from the dark valley to an elevated plain.
- The H of hope challenges us to hold our eyes higher, calling for a conscious decision to divert our attention from present problems and raise our eyes above the circumstances.
- The God who knows the stars by name knows the predicament of His people.
- When despondency threatens and we are uncertain of our future, we need to stop and remind ourselves that God sits "enthroned above the circle of the earth."

Thoughts to Journal

- Write out the H of Hope.
- What telephone poles are blocking your path?
- Identify the *what ifs* that haunt you.
- Where is your focus during the day—what thoughts are most prevalent?
- Are you like the Israelites sitting by the streams of Babylon, weeping for what once was?
- The God who knows the stars by name knows your plight. List every detail of your brokenness and acknowledge that God thoroughly knows you and the details you listed.
- "The answer to fading hope is not found in solved problems but in changed focus." How can you change your focus?

CHAPTER 4

How the "H" of Hope Sustained Me

The adoption process was about to end. We were sitting in the airport, waiting for the Northwest Orient plane to deliver our five-and-a-half-month-old daughter. The delayed flight finally arrived and the last to disembark were six dark-haired baby girls in white blouses with red embroidered roses. Weary chaperones handed their precious cargo to eager parents.

Stacey Joy came into our lives with a wail and a will. When she was placed in my waiting arms, we were told that Stacey cried for the entire twenty-four-hour flight, but our new daughter did nothing but sleep on the long ride home from the airport. I smugly assured myself that all she needed was her mother's touch. I was quickly proven wrong.

Stacey Joy joined an older brother, Shane, who was two. Shane had been a dream baby, eating and sleeping, sleeping and cooing, and sleeping some more. Stacey did not follow suit. Oh, she ate and she cooed—it was the sleep part she couldn't master. We assumed her internal clock needed adjustment so we gave her time. Six months later we realized that Stacey had a time clock all her own and there was no way we were going to reset it. She was adorable, but she was awake—a lot.

Our family continued to grow. Two years and two months after Stacey's arrival, I gave birth to a second son, Corey. Then we became foster parents and adopted our fourth child, David. Next, we suffered a failed pregnancy with twin girls, Joy and Peace. The adoption of Bethany a year later completed our family—three boys and two girls, ranging in age from ten to newborn. Our house was filled with the giggles and tattles, joys and challenges of five young children.

When the older three were teenagers, we enjoyed the inevitable whirlwind of friends, unannounced dinner guests, and sleepless slee-povers. Eventually our hosting expanded to include visiting girlfriends, wall to wall sleeping bags, and shower schedules posted on the door of our only bathroom.

Since our children were close in age, the marriages of our oldest three came one after the other, as did the grandchildren. Our children were in each other's weddings and Stacey made sure Bethany knew that when she married, Stacey would be her maid of honor. We all attended the same church, hiked and picked apples together, and shared family dinners. We celebrated each other's birthdays with round-table con-versations about what we appreciated about the birthday person. We laughed a lot, talked a lot, played a lot and were crazy together. We had three grandchildren in less than two years and were awaiting the births of two more. I fondly refer to this time as our Camelot Years. Then Stacey's death changed everything.

Losing Stacey blasted an irreparable hole in our hearts. She was the pizzazz of our family—the party planner, the family communicator, the funny one, the drama queen, and the care giver. Stacey was our song, our laughter, our glue. Her death devastated us, individually and as a family unit. Our pain was compounded by the anguish of her husband, who lost his wife weeks before their fifth anniversary, and the sad confusion of their young daughter, only three years old.

I was shattered. My prayers were moans. I needed reminders to eat and drink. I couldn't read, couldn't think clearly. For the first time, I was a mother who couldn't comfort her own children. I felt like my usefulness was over, that I would never again have anything to contribute, never again have a passion to teach. I fluctuated between desperation and despondency. And yet, in that stupor of grief, God's grace lured my eyes upward, compelling me to hold them higher.

Tenaciously, without cooperative emotions or enlightened understanding, I forced my eyes to look to the heavens, to the One who created and ruled my personal world. It was there that the threat of despair was beaten back. I forced my eyes above the empty chair at our family table, beyond the phone that didn't ring, past the screaming silence of her absence.

I saw Stacey alive. I heard her infectious laugh and imagined her delight in amazing heavenly discoveries. I envisioned her reunion with her beloved Grandpa. I understood time in God's dimension and calculated that if a day is as a thousand years[11] and I live to be a hundred, I would see Stacey in four and a half minutes. I could do that! I counted on the truth that in all things, even in this horrible thing, God works for my blessing[12] and insisted there was blessing I could not see.

Through clenched teeth and unstoppable tears, I acknowledged that my way was not hidden from the Lord, nor was my cause disregarded by Him. I could not fathom His understanding but *when I lifted my eyes*, Isaiah's promise was made real in my life: "Those who hope in the Lord will renew their strength. They will soar on wings like eagles; they will run and not grow weary, they will walk and not be faint."[13]

It's been fourteen years now, and I still cry, still hurt, and still long for Stacey's company. But I have learned to walk again, on legs made strong through the discipline of looking higher, above the place I live. There are days when I run. There are even days when I soar— not because I no longer feel pain, but because I choose to lift my eyes. This is why I offer you the H of hope. I know it works. Hold your eyes higher.

---

[11] Psalm 90:4

[12] Romans 8:28

[13] Isaiah 40:27-31

For Personal Reflection

Points to Ponder

- I fluctuated between desperation and despondency. And yet, in that stupor of grief, God's grace pulled my eyes upward, compelling me to hold them higher.
- Tenaciously, without cooperative emotions or enlightened understanding, I forced my eyes to look to the heavens, to the One who created and ruled my personal world.
- There are days when I run. There are even days when I soar— not because I no longer feel pain, but because I choose to lift my eyes.

Thoughts to Journal

- What shattering experience brought you to read this book?
- Do the math found in Psalm 90:4: a thousand years are like a day. If you live to be 100, how long will your pain endure?
- Are you willing to lift your eyes higher?

O

CHAPTER 5

The "O" Path

I rushed around the corner with a basket of laundry on my hip and bumped into my husband. There he stood, arms folded, staring at the storage shelves across from my washer. I knew I was in trouble. I could tell from his stance that his oft-repeated speech on *purging* was about to come forth. I didn't have long to wait.

Over the years I've collected seasonal decorations for spring, summer, fall and winter (in addition to Christmas décor) and must admit, many of these items no longer leave the shelf. They sit alongside mementos from our kids' mission trips—a plate from Russia, a vase from Malaysia, a hand-carved mug from Mexico. On the same shelves are teapots with cracked spouts, shells garnered from the seashore, and a random collection of unique serving pieces. And then there are the boxes of candles—new candles, half-burned candles, bent candles, discolored candles—more candles than any number of blackouts could demand. I don't *intend* to save all this stuff. It just accumulates, piece by piece, and as it does my husband continues to ask, "Why don't you get rid of this stuff?"

Why don't I get rid of it? Why do I save a dozen generic vases from long gone floral arrangements? Why do I keep clothes in the back of my closet that are two sizes too small? Why do I store a box of fabric under the bed, when I no longer sew? I'm sure you have asked yourself similar questions.

The outmoded treasures on our shelves and end tables no longer hold their sparkle, but sit there because we won't part with them. They take up space that could accommodate something fresh and lovely, but we dust them off and set them back in place. There's an uncanny fear in parting with things we love, but not only are our homes filled with sentimental keepsakes—so are our hearts. And if we find it difficult to purge our homes, how much harder is it to purge our hearts?

We file unfulfilled plans and stale dreams under *Someday*. We open the folder but are no longer inspired by what once excited us. With no expectation, we simply close the file drawer. Many of those files should be shredded, but *Deferred Hope* has introduced his friend, *Lethargy*. Unchallenged, our hearts have grown indifferent and hope has inadvertently dwindled. We need revival and find it on the next path—the O of hope. Open your heart to God's opportunities. This path is critical. If we don't walk it and surrender the past, God may wrest our dream from us.

Lari's Dashed Dream

Long before I met her, Lari cherished a vision for mission work in India, even with her responsibilities as a single mother. When she was a teenager she didn't know the Lord, but she did know the young man who took advantage of her and left her to face pregnancy alone. Lari moved into a Christian home for single pregnant women and met Jesus Christ. Her faith and the child within her grew as she nourished both, and when her son arrived, he was born to a devoted Christian mother. Lari raised Tanner to honor the Lord and, when he was only three, she brought him to India on a three-month mission trip. Her heart was seared with a love for the Indian people and she returned to college to prepare to become a missionary, never questioning where her assignment would be. Lari's determination was fueled by her passion for the Lord and her love for India. After years of full-time mothering, full-time work, and part-time college, Lari graduated and pursued her dream. Painfully, every door shut. Every door but one, that is. There was an opportunity to serve in Budapest, Hungary.

This was not the direction for which Lari had prepared. Her prayers, her study, her dreams were all for India—this could *not* be God. Didn't He put India in her heart? Her every thought through the long waiting period was for the Indian people. Budapest? For years she had patiently, methodically put the pieces in place to serve in India. Her hope plummeted, but Lari knew Jeremiah 29:11.

She knew that God's plans are not to harm us but to prosper us and give us hope and a future. The problem was, Lari was now unsure of His plans and she questioned her future, her God, and her heart. It was agonizing to take the dream of India off the shelf where it had been nurtured and treasured.

In the midst of her confusion, Lari acknowledged God's sovereignty and gradually opened her heart to the opportunity that made no sense. As she released what she had believed was God's will and yielded to Him, the Lord led her steps and equipped her with everything necessary for His assignment in Budapest. Lari could feel the dimming embers of hope rekindle.

She and her seven-year-old son moved to Hungary, where Lari worked on the streets of Budapest. She studied the language as she served at a home for single mothers and ministered among gypsy women. She embraced the Lord's opportunity and a beautiful thing happened. Somewhere between the street work and the gypsy camp Lari met Mike, an American missionary pilot.

Today, Lari has a Godly husband, Tanner has a devoted father and Mike has a wife who shares his vision. They added two more sons to their family and now minister in Asia. It's worth noting, that in all Mike's years of service, he never visited India. What would be their story if Lari had clung to her dream and not opened her heart to God's opportunity?

What dreams do we need to release? What will God show us if we open our hearts? What would be our story if Peter had not opened his heart to fresh vision from God?

Open Hearts Discover Opportunity

The apostle Peter's invitation to embark on a groundbreaking opportunity caused tremendous inner turmoil. He was a man of convictions, based on years of religious training, and he could not comprehend the prospect before him. At least he asked the right question—could this be from God? When trust won out, Peter embarked on a remarkable God-venture.

Born a Jew, Peter scrupulously followed the law and when he acknowledged Jesus as Messiah, he followed Him with the same tenacity. Peter's zeal increased after the outpouring of the Holy Spirit on

Pentecost and his ministry bore fruit—people came to faith and the sick were healed.

When Peter was traveling throughout Palestine he received a vision that challenged his thinking and called him to alter his precious convictions. Thankfully, he responded to the Holy Spirit's prompting. Leaving the comfort of familiarity, Peter opened his heart to a new opportunity and accepted an invitation to the home of a Gentile, a Roman centurion named Cornelius.

The unorthodox nature of Peter's visit was disclosed in his first words to the people gathered in Cornelius's home, "You are well aware that it is against our law for a Jew to associate with a Gentile or visit him."[14]

Up to this point, Peter's ministry was full and satisfying, God-blessed and God-directed—but restricted to the Jews. Peter opened his heart to God's opportunity and embraced a fresh vision. He told the Gentile crowd, "God has shown me that I should not call any man impure or unclean. So when I was sent for, I came without raising any objection...."[15] That day the gift of the Holy Spirit was poured out on the Gentiles and they were baptized in the name of Jesus.[16]

Against this backdrop, Peter penned these words in his first letter: "But you are a chosen people, a royal priesthood, a holy nation, a people belonging to God, that you may declare the praises of him who called you out of darkness into his wonderful light. Once you were not a people, but now you are the people of God: once you had not received mercy, but now you have received mercy."[17]

Peter did not let his treasured beliefs keep him from stepping into God's path of opportunity. If he had not opened his heart, the honor of ushering in that royal priesthood would belong to another. Not many of us will have a Peter-like opportunity of world-wide magnitude, but we will have opportunities that affect our little piece of the world.

Unexpected Blessing

One small starter home and four children under the age of eight were the only excuses I needed to not host our Friday night meeting. My husband and I belonged to a fast-growing group of enthusiastic believers who met in alternating homes for worship, fellowship, and prayer and soon it would be our turn to host. Initially I was excited, even expectant, but the more I thought about it, the more my excitement shriveled and my excuses swelled. My husband, however, would not be deterred so when the appointed Friday evening came, he squeezed chairs into every space. One by one, each chair filled and our living room was packed to capacity. That night a little bit of heaven infiltrated our home.

We experienced rich fellowship and the group continued to grow. I wish I could say I no longer worried about fitting everyone in the living room, but each time our turn came around so did my doubts and each time we hosted, our numbers increased and every seat was taken. How could a living room already filled to capacity accommodate more guests? My husband and I simply removed more and more furniture.

Taking out one old rocker made room for two kitchen chairs. Wheeling out the television allowed for three more seats. The magazine rack, antique jugs, potted plant and baby swing all had to go. We surrendered familiar comforts to make room for God's greater purposes. What was well-ordered and carefully positioned, acquiesced to the unfamiliar and uncomfortable. This was not only true of our house, it was true of our hearts. Our God-in-a-box and religious traditions moved aside when worship flowed from full hearts and spiritual gifts manifested themselves. We not only made room for God's people, we made room for Him. When we put aside the limits of our experience and opened our hearts to God's opportunity, the blessings overflowed. My inflexibility could have kept us from venturing down the path God had for us. In opening my heart, not only was I blessed, but so were others.

Safety or Adventure?

When God entrusts us with visions and dreams, they are not ours to mold according to our understanding. They are His to unfold in His time, according to His wisdom. He often inspires dreams for reasons we don't understand and when He brings us down an unexpected path we have a choice. We can yield to our fears and seal the door of our hearts or, in faith, we can throw the door open and invite the Spirit to accomplish purposes known only to Him. Every twist, diversion, or detour leads to a future He alone sees. Hiding behind the safety of closed doors will rob us of the joy of obedience.

What if Lari had not let go of her dream of India? What if Peter had not accepted the Gentiles? What if I allowed fear to close my home and heart? In each of these three journeys, the familiar had to be released before the new could be embraced. Precious dreams that had been stored on personal shelves were surrendered to make space for new exploits. Only then were incredible paths of adventure and blessing realized.

When Stacey died, our family portrait shifted, our dynamic was altered. We were no longer who we once were. The snapshot was marred. Far from being open, my heart shut tight and fear of the unknown threatened to confine me.

Refusing to be Boxed In

When fear is permitted to triumph over trust, it boxes us in and jeopardizes God's blessing in our lives. The lid comes off when we believe that God means it when He says, "I know the plans I have for you... plans to prosper you... not to harm you, plans to give you hope and a future" (Jeremiah 29:11). God's plans always make us more, not less. They increase our capacity, our joy, our hope. We can trust a God like that.

The sides of our boxes fall when we agree with the psalmist that "all the ways of the Lord are loving and faithful...."[18] Trusting in His love and faithfulness will displace fear and allow us to follow Him with confidence.[19] No longer will concern for personal safety or comfort deafen us to God-breathed opportunities.

Believing that God created us to do good works He's already prepared for us[20] lifts us out of the box. Because God has a plan, we have a destiny. The God of love has uniquely created us for purposes He designed. Trusting that truth liberates us.

Cleaning House

God's plans need space and freedom to grow. We accommodate them by moving out cumbersome, comfortable furniture and ridding ourselves of emotional clutter. If there's no indication God is presently active in former plans, it's time to clean house and make room. If our dreams no longer stir passion or have become weighty and cause more anxiety than joy, they are taking up valuable space. If resentment, disappointment or past failures are lounging in the recesses of our hearts, we need to release them. Dead end plans, stagnant dreams and coddled self-pity debilitate hope. Removing their clutter will make room for the new.

God's opportunities are waiting for open hearts to accommodate them. He will use the gifts He uniquely gave us, some of which are yet to be discovered. His plans will satisfy our deepest longings and send us on better ventures than we can imagine. Rather than being robbed of God's destiny for our future, let's anticipate His direction. His purposes will stretch us but they also assure blessing.

When we relinquish stale plans and personal opinions about how life should look, we permit God to plant fresh dreams in our hearts. Let's make space for His agenda, His work, His people—His blessing. When we do, we will see flickering hope once again fan into flame.

What will our story be when we open our hearts to God's opportunities?

---

14 Acts 10:28a
15 Acts 10:28b-29
16 Acts 10:44-48
17 I Peter 2:9-10

18 Psalm 25:10
19 Psalm 25:12
20 Ephesians 2:10

For Personal Reflection

Points to Ponder

- We need personal revival and find it when we Open our Hearts to God's Opportunities.
- What dreams do we need to release? What will God show us if we open our hearts?
- When God entrusts us with visions and dreams, they are His to unfold in His time, according to His wisdom.
- God's opportunities are waiting for open hearts to accommodate them.

Thoughts to Journal

- Write out the O of Hope.
- What cherished dreams are you clinging to that should be released?
- Have you considered that God may have a better plan for you?
- Refuse to let fear triumph over trust. Dream big—imagine scenarios God could have for you and then acknowledge that His plans are beyond your imagination.
- Make space for God's agenda. Start cleaning house today.

—O—

CHAPTER 6

How the "O" of Hope Sustained Me

Early in our marriage God clearly indicated a path to parenthood for me and my husband. We moved forward with anticipation and the peace of being in His will. Then plans derailed—and I crashed. We were at the last stage of the adoption process for our first child. Following the social worker's home visit, he would fly back to his office and send us a picture of our Korean daughter. Was I excited? *Yes* would be an extreme understatement.

I had not quickly become pregnant so, rather than follow the doctor's advice to give it two years, my husband and I prayerfully decided to move up our plans for adoption. Instead of adopting *someday* we would start the process now. We inquired at many agencies but when I opened the letter from Holt International Children's Services, I wept. My husband and I both knew, with unquestioned certainty, that this was God's path for us.

The adoption wait was nine months and I did what every first-time mother does. I bought a library of books with descriptions and pictures so I could follow our daughter's development. As she grew in a womb across the globe she also grew in the chamber of my heart. Then, to our surprise, we conceived. Our social worker was scheduled for a home visit and we couldn't wait to tell him the good news—we were going to have two babies.

His response was not what we anticipated. As he sat in our living room explaining the agency's policy, my joy melted into a flood of hormonal tears. We didn't know they would not place a baby in a home where there was a pregnancy. We argued our case. Didn't they understand that God clearly indicated we were to adopt through them? There was no question of His leading. Surely they would bend the rules for our situation! But they wouldn't. We could reactivate our application when our biological baby turned one.

I mourned. Perhaps only an adoptive mother can understand the depth of my grief, but it was as if I miscarried. My sorrow even eclipsed the joy of my pregnancy. For a long time we told no one I was expecting, but as my abdomen swelled so did my happiness. I was able to accept my disappointment as God's detour and, one year after our son was born, we reopened our adoption application.

Before our son Shane's second birthday, our daughter was born on the other side of the world. Stacey Joy was five-and-a-half-months old when she arrived from Korea. Her name means *renewal of joy* and that she was. We had not misunderstood God's leading. He simply chose an alternate route and in doing so He doubled our joy. We had been on the right path—we simply hit an unanticipated detour. This was an important lesson to learn because many years later my survival depended on it.

My husband and I served thirty-four years in one church. Our children were dedicated, baptized, and married there. We cherished sweet relationships and created volumes of memories. At the twenty-four-year mark, Rich was invited to be Pastor of Congregational Care and we immediately accepted. It was the fulfillment of God's call on our lives—early in our marriage we knew Rich was destined for the ministry but didn't realize the wait would be so long.

Our enthusiasm exploded. Dreams and goals filled our conversation and kept us awake at night, but in only three years things began to break down. Our church was no longer a place of refuge but filled with suspicion, rocking on the brink of division. In a short while the friends who attended us in Stacey's death, avoided us. The senior pastor left amid conflict-ridden controversy. Rumors flew and people fled. A new pastor came but the church continued to dwindle. After two years my husband was abruptly released from his position. Thirty-four years of dreams, struggles and service were dismissed in one night. Thirty-four years!

Obstacles to continuing in the ministry marched across our minds: the recession, my husband's age, his lack of formal seminary training. Technology advanced during Rich's years in ministry, prohibiting a return to his former field. An aging mother and handicapped son locked us into our present location. Rich pored over online job sights, contacted associates and ministries, sent out resumes, and even applied for manual labor positions. Our mortgage, taxes and living expenses demanded payment. We were without a church and without the friends we had served beside.

The decision to release dreams and goals which were the substance of our lives for more than thirty-four years, was painful and confusing. Letting go of dreams that once inspired and sustained us was heart wrenching, but releasing them also saved us. We opened our hearts to

God and allowed Him to clean house. We invited Him to do whatever He pleased and, once again, He proved that He "is able to do immeasurably more than we can ask or imagine."[21] We were without a plan; He was not.

Today my husband serves as Pastor of Congregational Care in a thriving, healthy church. He prays with people in the early morning hours before their surgery and meets with men in the evening at the end of their work day. He is busy and fulfilled. But that is not the victory in our story. The victory is that an open heart became an open door for God's opportunities and hope persevered through the darkness.

---

[21] Ephesians 3:20

—○—

For Personal Reflection

Points to Ponder

- I was able to accept my disappointment as God's detour.
- Letting go of dreams that once inspired and sustained us was heart wrenching, but releasing them also saved us.
- We invited God to do whatever He pleased and, once again, He proved that He "is able to do immeasurably more than we can ask or imagine." We were without a plan; He was not.

Thoughts to Journal

- How did you assume your life would play out?
- Can you recall a time when God gave you (or someone you know) something better than what was planned?
- List at least five unexpected blessings from God.

—O—

P

CHAPTER 7

The "P" Path

By nature, I am an orderly person. I'm a maker of lists who keeps a list of my lists, sad but true. It's part of my God-given DNA and I am most comfortable when organized. My first child cooperated with my schedule. My second child had her own schedule. My third child broke anything that resembled a schedule. My fourth child—what's a schedule?

Our second and fourth children were adopted, as was our seventh. Early on, my husband and I completed enough applications from various organizations to know that agencies want adoptions to succeed. In an effort to prevent adoption failures, they ask pointed questions about the challenges prospective families feel they can or cannot meet. We answered many such questions. Blind? Yes. Deaf? Maybe. Racial diversity? Yes. Physical limitations? Yes. Emotional problems? Not sure. Hyperactivity? Definitely not!

David came to our home as a foster child when our other children were seven, six and three. At the age of three months, he had just been released from his second hospitalization for severe malnutrition. He was listless. His cry was too weak to be heard and his eyes held no life. A few weeks after coming to us, an infant psychiatrist visited and assured us that David would thrive in the loving atmosphere of our home. Six months passed and I anxiously awaited her follow-up assessment because I wasn't seeing the progress she predicted. She glanced down at David lying in his playpen and her eyes locked with mine. I can still hear her hushed words, "I'm sorry. I was wrong."

At two David could barely hold a sitting position, didn't speak, couldn't walk—and became available for adoption. At two and a half we signed the papers and made him ours. At two and three-quarters he learned to walk and took off running. The hyperactivity, with which I openly admitted I could not cope, took up permanent residence in our home.

I don't remember the incidences that prompted it, but I clearly remember aimlessly riding the dark streets one night. Tired and miserable, I was devoid of hope. The spark was gone. With tears spilling down my cheeks as I drove, I pleaded, "Lord, you made me. You know I'm an organized person. What are you doing to me? You know I don't function well in chaos. Change things! Calm this child. Give him a quiet spirit. I'm *begging* you."

For the next hour I meandered through back streets and rehearsed the mayhem in my life, as if God wasn't aware. I told Him about the bushel of apples tossed down the cellar steps, about the toys floating in the fish tank, about the outings our family missed, about David's resistance to eating, about his falling, his crying, and the brevity of his naps, about my weariness and my husband's overtime. Finally depleted, I became still and, in the stillness, three inescapable truths came into focus.

The first was that I was in love with a little boy who would forever alter our lifestyle, a child who would never speak and would require medication to quiet down. Secondly, I knew that God wanted him in our home, having slipped David in the back door without revealing his hyperactivity until he was already ours. And, thirdly, I knew my survival depended on gripping God's promises and holding them dearer than my problem. The "P" of hope would be my salvation—Ponder the Positive, not the Problems.

The Path our Thoughts Take

When our thoughts follow their natural inclination, they gravitate to our troubles. Left unchecked, this default setting invites us to obsess over our problems. We examine them from every angle, turning them over and over again in our minds. We waste an untold number of words and far too much time rehearsing the details of our situation. We compile a list of solutions and then, as a reflection of our spiritual maturity, we pray the problems, taking care to mention the merits of our proposed solutions. One of the quickest ways to devastate hope is to let this pattern go unchecked. When our mind dwells only on our problems, we are blinded to the enormity of God's promises and the goodness of His nature.

It is not that our problems aren't valid—the bills are coming, the child is in rehab, the husband is distant, the car does clunk, the lump is in the breast. We cannot, must not, allow the weight of our troubles to push the love of God and the certainty of His Word into the recesses of our mind. As true as our troubles are, there is a greater Truth.

The Greater Truth

When obstacles overwhelm and appear insurmountable, the greater truth is, "You, O Lord, keep my lamp burning; my God turns my darkness into light. With your help I can advance against a troop; with my God *I can scale a wall*."[22]

Everything looks grim when we're inundated with problems. A truth greater than our challenges is that God's goodness is waiting for us. The psalmist says, "How great is your goodness, which you have *stored up* for those who fear you, which you bestow in the sight of men on those who take refuge in you."[23]

When we are weary and worn down by the urgency of our circumstances, the truth is, "The Sovereign Lord is my strength; he makes my feet like the feet of a deer, *he enables me to go on the heights*."[24]

Pain isolates us and loneliness intensifies our fears, but God says, "I am the Lord, your God, who takes hold of your right hand and says to you, 'Do not fear; *I will help you*.'"[25]

When truth retains its rightful place, even in the dark times, it reminds us that God is faithful and will provide a way out so we can stand,[26] that nothing is too hard for our limitless God,[27] and that, in ways we can't understand, God will work out our troubles to bring us blessing.[28]

Which truth will we choose to fill our minds? If we default to our problems, we allow our hope to further shrivel. Pondering the positive—God's character, God's faithfulness, God's words—will nourish hope and make it strong, but it requires a conscious decision. The psalmist David made that decision and, as he pondered the higher truth in the midst of recurring calamities, his hope endured.

King David's Choice

David suffered greater challenges than most of us. He was humiliated, threatened and hunted. He sinned spectacularly and bore the weight of the consequences. As a warrior, he led rebel forces and commanded Israel's army. Friends deserted him and, worse yet, betrayed him. As a king, his son attempted to overthrow and murder him. His troubles were overwhelming and could have consumed him, but David chose to ponder the positive.

Psalm 56 was written when the Philistine army pursued and eventually captured David. Without minimizing his trouble, he poured out his heart to God and recounted his predicament, pleading, "Be merciful to me, O God, for men hotly pursue me; all day long they press their attack. My slanderers pursue me all day long; many are attacking me in their pride."[29] Even though his situation was dire, in the next verse David immediately fixed his thoughts on God, "When I am afraid, I will trust in you. In God, whose word I praise, in God I trust; I will not be afraid. What can mortal man do to me?"[30]

When David was a fugitive, he fled for his life and hid in a cave. In the dark recesses he cried out to God, "I am in the midst of lions; I lie among ravenous beasts—men whose teeth are spears and arrows, whose tongues are sharp swords."[31] Again, David made a pivotal decision. He wrote, "I will praise you, O Lord, among the nations; I will sing of you among the peoples. For great is your love, reaching to the heavens; your faithfulness reaches to the skies."[32]

David's son usurped his throne and sought to kill him. In great distress, David spilled out his misery to God, "My heart is in anguish within me; the terrors of death assail me. Fear and trembling have beset me; horror has overwhelmed me."[33] It would be reasonable for David to wallow in regret about the past or fixate on the dangers before him. Instead, in his hopeless hour, David centered his attention on God's goodness and love. He chose to magnify God's faithfulness and closed the psalm with these words: "Cast your cares on the Lord and he will sustain you; he will never let the righteous fall.... As for me, I trust in you."[34]

David's choice to focus on God's sufficiency did not alter his problems any more than the same choice would affect ours, but his decision instilled hope and his belief in God lightened the weight of his grief. How heavy is your load? Do you have actual or emotional enemies? Is someone attacking your position, your worth? Are you contending with an adversarial child or spouse? Are enemies (or friends) slandering you? How much are you carrying?

Choose What You Pack

We can relate to the allegorical picture of a traveler weighed down by the sack on his back because, like the burdened wanderer, we become bent over from the heaviness of our problems. Wearily, we come to the point of relinquishment, responding to Christ's invitation to cast our burdens on Him.[35]

How liberating to unpack our worries and lay each one before Him! We sincerely confess our inadequacy to carry such a load and thank Him for relieving us of our problems, professing His sufficiency to deal with them. As we leave the altar of relinquishment, two possible scenarios loom and both are problematic. In the first scenario, we cast a final, longing look at our problems and, before realizing it, we tenderly repack the burdens in our sack. The second alternative is that we resist the temptation and determine to not pick up that weight again, walking off lighter and happier. This sounds like the better choice, but actually both options can lead to despair.

The problem with the first scenario is obvious—we don't trust God to take care of things and continue to bear the weight ourselves. The problem with the second is subtle. A sack that is empty leaves space for new problems—or we may slink back at a future date to reclaim those we half-heartedly relinquished. Since our sack is like a vacuum that refuses to remain unfilled, the most important step in surrendering our burden to God is to purposefully refill our sacks. In place of personal worries we can choose God's assurances.

Making God's promises our constant companion is the antidote to despair. Holding them close, keeps us from obsessing over our troubles. Think of King David's example. He unloaded his sack before the Lord but held fast to the higher truth of God's character, ability and promises, thereby preparing himself for future challenges. We can do the same, but only when we deliberately choose to hold truth close by pondering it and prioritizing it. It's the choice between freedom and imprisonment.

When problems are our primary focus, we empower them to dictate our mood, behavior and decisions, equipping them to lock us in prisons of despair. What we ponder can change that, even when circumstances stubbornly remain the same. My friend Edwin spent much time in a literal prison and saw this principal work, making his story one of triumph.

Behind Bars but Free

When he was a young man growing up in Paterson, New Jersey, Edwin was one tough hombre. He earned a reputation as a formidable boxer, but his fighting wasn't restricted to the ring. When Edwin walked the city streets people got out of his way. He was an intimidating man, in stature and demeanor. The rougher he became, the greater his following and the fiercer his reputation. His induction into a gang was a natural progression and Edwin earned his way up through the ranks with cruelty and brutality. Within five years he was named Gang General, second in command.

He was in and out of jail and prison, but even behind bars, Edwin ruled with a cadre of loyal admirers who revered him. He was a mean man with mean men following him. In their eyes, Edwin could do no wrong and they had his back, protecting him, watching out for him, and jumping to do what he asked. When he served time, no one touched him. Other gangs respected him—he was *the man*.

Ten years of gang violence and drug abuse took a toll on Edwin. He was worn out and too tired to sustain gang life any longer. He knew he would pay a high price for leaving, but he wanted out and said so. The exit beating he endured almost cost him his life. Blows from wooden bats left black and blue bruises over his entire body. He suffered a broken arm and leg. Stab wounds punctured him from head to foot. He had twenty-two stitches on his chin alone. Six weeks in the hospital mended Edwin's body, but did nothing to soften his heart. He remained a hard, angry man, which is why there was no reasonable explanation for his church attendance—except the faithful prayers of his mother.

Edwin began to lead a dual life. On Sundays he appeared to be a man on the road to redemption, but the rest of the week he wrestled demons of anger and addiction. One day, in downtown Paterson, the two paths intersected.

Throughout Edwin's history of aggression, there was one line he never crossed. He would not harm a woman. That's why his actions on that ill-fated Saturday afternoon surprised him. Edwin needed a fix. The money in his pocket propelled him down the city sidewalk, on a mission to satisfy his craving. He walked past a woman and noticed her gold necklace. Without forethought, he reached out, wrenched the chain from her neck and took off running. The police were on his tail in no time but Edwin knew every alley in Paterson. He was almost home free—just one leap over a fence and he would escape. But he couldn't leap; he couldn't even move. He heard music. Worship songs filled the air for Edwin's ears alone. Before he knew what he was doing he stepped out on the sidewalk and flagged down the police, surrendering himself and the gold chain.

With Edwin's past record, the fact that he turned himself in did nothing to soften his sentence and he faced another prison term. Previously, Edwin counted on his gang for protection, but this time they were cause for fear. Those who once guarded him were now enemies who scorned him. Rather than gang reverence, he faced gang hostility. Edwin's status had changed and he knew danger lurked behind the prison bars. Despair threatened, but Edwin's fledgling faith began to grow.

He wrestled with regret and guilt over a lifetime of crime and cruelty. The memories of his exit beating were still fresh and Edwin considered the menacing possibilities before him—bullying, beatings, rape, death. If he entertained fear, it would eat him up. He could not spend his days pondering the negative. Thankfully, Edwin had become a fully devoted disciple of Jesus Christ. Armed with his newfound faith, he pondered the positive and held fast to God's promises. Rather than shrivel, his hope flourished behind prison bars. Edwin tells it best.

To walk in faith in prison is not a battle anyone wins alone. I counted on the Holy Spirit to help me think and live in new ways. Gang members mocked and threatened me but the Lord used Bible studies and chapel services to make me stronger and stronger. My situation was terrifying. Three high ranking gang bangers had a hit out on me. Death was my greatest fear but instead of dwelling on what men could do, I focused on the Word and the resurrection power of Jesus Christ.

When my eyes were on my danger and the hatred of men, I was tempted to retaliate, but the Holy Spirit helped me think in new ways, reminding me of Scriptures. I knew that the One in me was greater than he who is in the world.[36] I knew that nothing could separate me from God's love.[37] He showed me in a dream that I had a shield of protection to rely on.[38]

There were many difficulties and multitudes of issues to work through, patterns in my life that had to change. Sometimes I felt like I was crazy, but God promised me victory.[39] I kept pulling my mind back to Him and His Word. By the end of my sentence the guards, prisoners and gang members gave up tormenting me and some even asked for prayer. To God be all the glory, because the glory is in *His* story.

Though physically in prison, facing a seemingly hopeless situation, Edwin forced his thoughts upward. He pondered the positive promises of God rather than allowing the threat of negative circumstances to consume him. It is no different for us. Whatever fears imprison us, we can renew hope by choosing to ponder the positive.

—P—

The Practice of Pondering

Selah is a Hebrew word found seventy-two times in the Psalms. In essence, it means *pause and calmly think about that*. It first appears in Psalm 3:1-2:

> O Lord, how many are my foes! How many rise up against me! Many are saying of me, "God will not deliver him." *Selah*

Pause and calmly think about that. Are your foes—those obstacles and persons who come against you—many? Do you feel threatened, outnumbered, fearful? Now read verses 3-4:

> But you are a shield around me, O Lord; you bestow glory on me and lift up my head. To the Lord I cry aloud, and he answers me from his holy hill. *Selah*

Did you notice the significance of the first word? *But* trumps the previous two verses. God is a shield around me. He bestows glory on me. He lifts my head. He answers me. Selah—pause and calmly think about *that*.

The psalm ends with this assurance:

> I lie down and sleep; I wake again, because the Lord sustains me. I will not fear the tens of thousands drawn up against me on every side....From the Lord comes deliverance. May your blessing be on your people. *Selah*[40]

Peaceful sleep, sustaining grace, courage, deliverance, blessing—pause and calmly think about that.

We choose what we will ponder. When we pause and think about God's goodness and grace, we nourish our understanding of His nature and how He acts. This causes hope to swell.

What we feed grows—in the animal world, in the plant world, and in the spiritual world. Fear and worry cannot thrive if they are not fed. They are weakened and can no longer overtake our minds and strangle our hope. Let's refuse to rehash the details of our problems and choose to pause and calmly think about the positive assurances of Scripture. As we *selah* God's truth, it will become central to our thinking and hope will rise, displacing its enemies.

Let's change our default setting. Let's turn truth over and over in our minds, examine God's character from every angle, and share our discoveries with each other. Our problems may challenge hope, but God's promises challenge our problems.

Ponder the positive, not the problems and live in the hope that He gladly gives. *Selah.*

---

22 Psalm 18:28-29 [italics added]

23 Psalm 31:19 [italics added]

24 Habakkuk 3:19 [italics added]

25 Isaiah 41:13 [italics added]

26 I Corinthians 10:13

27 Genesis 18:14, Jeremiah 32:17, 27

28 Romans 8:28

29 Psalm 56:1

30 Psalm 56:3,4

31 Psalm 57:4

32 Psalm 57:9-10

33 Psalm 55:4-5

34 Psalm 55:22

35 Matthew 11:28

36 1 John 4:4

37 Romans 8:38-39

38 Psalm 144:2

39 Psalm 18:35;1 Cor.15:57

40 Psalm 3:5,7-8

For Personal Reflection

Points to Ponder

- I knew my survival depended on gripping God's promises and holding them dearer than my problem. The "P" of hope would be my salvation.
- As true as our troubles are, there is a greater Truth.
- *Selah*, pause and calmly think about that.
- Pondering the positive—God's character, God's faithfulness, God's words—will nourish hope and make it strong, but it requires a conscious decision.
- Whatever fears imprison us, we can renew hope by choosing to ponder the positive.

Thoughts to Journal

- Write out the P Path of Hope.
- What is the default setting of your mind—problems or possibilities? What can you do to increase positive input in your thought life?
- What are the disposable items in your sack?
- The prison of your circumstance cannot imprison your thoughts. What has you chained? Claim your freedom.
- Start pondering the positive today—record one of God's promises on an index card, in a journal, or in your phone. Create a collection of promises and read them often.

CHAPTER 8

How the "P" of
Hope Sustained Me

How could I ponder the positive when my daughter's death had plunged me into the negative? I saw no light, only loss. My saving grace was my confidence in God's character and respect for His sovereignty. Bit by bit, revelations of His goodness formed thoughts of gratitude that became my testimony. Pondering those thoughts rescued me.

As we drove to the funeral home to make arrangements, I choked out the words, "I am so grateful for the privilege of being the mother who mourns for Stacey Joy." God knew she would live only thirty years and, although He could have placed her in any adoptive family, He gave her to us. I was very aware that another woman could be grieving Stacey's death, but I was chosen—and honored to be so. Not, *why me?* but the greater truth—*Yes, me!*

In the days before the funeral, friends streamed through our home. They were caring, sensitive, generous; I was numb. I appreciated the sympathy cards that contained handwritten Bible verses because I didn't have the wherewithal to pick up the Bible. I clearly remember sitting on the sofa in a stupor thinking, "I am so thankful I have Randy Alcorn's books in me!" I had read three of his novels[1] in which he wrote descriptions of heaven that exploded my understanding and enthralled my heart. Now, though I sat in mourning, I did not envision Stacey as dead, but alive in her new home, with all the excitement of discovery I had read about in those books. Not, *she's gone* but the greater truth—*She's there*!

When Stacey was a child, a little girl with three brothers, she prayed for God to give her a sister. Her prayers were answered doubly when I became pregnant with not one sister for Stacey, but two! We were ecstatic, soaring with expectation, but Joy and Peace were born three months early. From the delivery table, I looked across the room to see one daughter, then the other, take her last breath. It fell to my husband to tell our eight-year-old that her sisters were not coming home. Romans 8:28 became my mantra. As I laid in my hospital bed, I declared through gritted teeth, "Lord, you work all things together for the good of Stacey." Then I repeated the statement of faith for each member of our family. Now, twenty-two years later, I found myself doing the same thing, declaring by faith what I could not comprehend. Not, *how could you?* but the greater truth—*You can be trusted!*

Months after Stacey's death I clung to a book that confirmed God's trustworthiness. I had purchased the small, worn volume on my only visit to a used book shop fifteen years earlier. Since then, the antique book sat on my mantle as part of the décor, dusted but unopened. I ran my fingers over the gold embossed title on its faded green cover in wonder. I reverently considered its contents as a personal love letter from God, to be discovered at the time of my deepest sorrow. *The*

Potter's Wheel spoke truth greater than the truth of my pain. The words Ian Maclaren penned in 1904 reached a place within me that little else could touch:

> When one comes to the loss of young children—a sad perplexity—let it not be forgotten that they were given. If in the hour of bitterest grief it were asked of a bereaved mother whether she would prefer never to have possessed in order that she might never have lost—her heart would be very indignant. No little child has ever come from God and stayed a brief while in some human home—to return again to the Father—without making glad that home and leaving behind some trace of heaven... This short visit was not an incident: *it was a benediction.* The child departs, the remembrances, the influence, the associations remain... And if God recalls the child He lent, then let us thank Him for the loan, and consider that what made that child the messenger of God—its purity, modesty, trustfulness, gladness—has passed into our soul.[41]

Not, *why did you take Stacey?* but the greater truth—*Her life was a benediction; thank you for the loan.*

We choose which truths we treasure, which considerations we ponder. Thoughts come and go—will we dismiss them or embrace them? I am grateful to Robert Morris for the picture he paints in *Truly Free,*[42] comparing our minds to Grand Central Station. He writes, "Trains of thought pull in and out every second. Our destinations depend on which trains we board." He explains that the more often we board harmful, negative trains, the easier it becomes to ride them when we're lonely, depressed or tired.

So I ask, which trains will we board? We can't stop trains of thought from coming, but we can choose which ones we'll ride. The more often we make choices for positive thoughts that are based on Scripture, the easier those choices become.

In the Apostle Paul's words, "Whatever is true, whatever is noble, whatever is right, whatever is pure, whatever is lovely, whatever is admirable—if anything is excellent or praiseworthy—think about such things."[43] Selah that!

---

[41] Taken from The Potter's Wheel by Ian Maclaren, ©1904 (emphasis added).

[42] Taken from Truly Free by Robert Morris, copyright ©2015 Robert Morris. Used by permission of Thomas Nelson.

[43] Philippians 4:8

For Personal Reflection

Points to Ponder

- I saw no light, only loss. My saving grace was my confidence in God's character and respect for His sovereignty. Pondering those thoughts rescued me.
- "This short visit was not an incident: it was a benediction."
- The more often we board harmful, negative trains, the easier it becomes to ride them when we're lonely, depressed or tired. (Robert Morris)

Thoughts to Journal

- Are you in the place where your loss eclipses the light?
- List your fears. Beneath each one, write a greater truth.
- Identify which trains of thought you will refuse to board.

E

CHAPTER 9

The "E" Path

I pushed the last tack in the wall and stood back. The poster brightened my son's bedroom wall—I hoped it would also brighten his outlook. I stared at the bear peering out from behind a tree and smiled at the words printed beside him:

> Don't tell me that worrying doesn't help.
> The things I worry about never happen.

My son worried...a lot. I wasn't like that as a child. I simply expected things would somehow work out—and then life taught me otherwise. I learned that babies die at birth, drug addiction affects entire families, sickness is a thief, good intentions do not pay bills, and friends are not friends forever, despite what song lyrics claim. As life transpired I discovered that our family was not exempt from pain. Those things that happened to *someone else* were happening to us. I also learned that disappointment is fertile ground for cynicism. We laugh at the skeptical axioms of Murphy's Laws that tell us anything that can go wrong, will, but it isn't funny when that thinking affects how we view life.

Our imagination can readily turn a headache into a brain tumor, a quizzical look into an assault on our character, or an unforeseen expense into financial bankruptcy. We are quick to recall stories of similar situations that ended in disaster. But the bottom line is, pessimism is not compatible with faith in God.

I love Psalm 84:5, "Blessed are those whose strength is in you, who have set their hearts on pilgrimage." This tells me two important truths. First, my strength is in God, not myself and second, this life is a pilgrimage—I'm going *through*. And there's more. The next two verses say I can make my valley of weeping into a place of springs and I will go from strength to strength until I one day appear before God. Take that, Mr. Murphy!

In your valley of weeping, I cannot assure you that your headache is not a brain tumor, that the covert look you saw meant nothing, or that the bills will be paid when an envelope of money is slipped under your door. But I can assure you that you can face your problems with certainty and peace when you embrace the E of hope—Expect Grace.

In every challenge, we can expect God to give us the grace we need to meet that challenge and get through it victoriously, from strength to strength. Whatever mystery, trial, or threat lies before us, grace will meet us because God is present in it.

God's Presence

Human nature (and Murphy) tells us that if something can go wrong, it will. Faith tells us that if something goes wrong, God is there. This is true regardless of feelings or fears. Disappointment or disillusionment, rejection or regret does not remove God from our situation. Though we cannot put confidence in our circumstances, we *can* put our trust in the One who orchestrates them.

According to Paul, God is "the King eternal, immortal, invisible, the only God."[44] What comfort to know that God is eternal, before our past and ahead of our future—He is never absent. He is also immortal, not earthly, fallible or temporal—He never changes. Next, we read God is invisible. Really, Paul? Isn't that a bit obvious? Why not say that He is strong, sovereign or powerful?

After months of questioning God about this, He answered me in the midst of a boisterous wedding reception. It was the type of celebration where you can't hear the person next to you and resort to gesturing to have the salt passed. While isolated in the noisy crowd, sudden realization pounded in my heart and my soul hushed at the understanding that God was in this place, unseen but present. With startling revelation, I understood—He is the invisible God. I realized, with abrupt clarity, that to say God is invisible is to declare that He is present, but not seen. My feelings amid personal chaos mean nothing—God is there and, because He is present, I can expect grace. I will be carried. I will prevail. I will go from strength to strength. I will make it because He is present.

The psalmist understood this when he rhetorically asked God, "Where can I go from your presence? If I go up to the heavens, you are there; if I make my bed in the depths, you are there...If I say, 'Surely the darkness will hide me and the light become night around me,' even the darkness will not be dark to you; the night will shine like the day, for darkness is as light to you."[45] Whether we soar to the heavens, plunge to the depths, rise to the sun, cross oceans, or hide in darkness, *or cannot see Him*, God is present. He goes before us and occupies the space before we arrive.

What darkness shadows your space? What sorrows have shredded your happiness? What holes scar your life? Perhaps, like me, you lost a child. Maybe you've been betrayed or slandered or abandoned. Maybe you carry the pain of financial hardship or suffer physical challenges. Maybe your marriage isn't the happily-ever-after story you envisioned or the child you poured your life into, now scorns you. We are not alone with our shattered dreams, isolation, or rejection. God is there, in the deep waters that threaten to drown us and in the blazing flames lapping at our heels.[46] He is there when life explodes and blasts holes into the fabric of our existence.

Living with a Hole

When our daughter Stacey died I didn't think about holes. I only thought about pain. Slowly, I came to understand that her death left a deep hole—one that would never be filled and never close. It was now part of my life. It marked me. That realization both comforted and alarmed me. I became petrified of the hole. The full story follows, but I will tell you this much now—God was and is present in the hole.

Whatever their size or origin, holes are frightening. They disrupt the orderly lives we strive to lead with our routines for the present and plans for the future. The unexpected blasts that leave gaping chasms in our lives don't come with a handbook for hardship. We are left to pick through the debris, searching for something familiar while knowing everything is forever changed. Insecurity bullies hope from our hearts and sets up camp, welcoming fear.

This is the time to cry out to the One who is there, whether we feel Him or not. He is waiting and will rescue us—we will not be overcome. As we become aware of His presence, God moves us out of isolation and the fear that accompanies it. The agonizing holes, menacing waters, and threatening flames lose their terror because we are not alone. Grasping this truth and believing that we are precious to Him[47] will carry us through our trials.

What it Means to be Carried

Friends are a gift from God. They listen, they hold us, they bring us meals. Their value is immeasurable and their burden-sharing priceless, but they are limited. They can't carry us. The old spiritual tells a timeless truth, "Nobody knows the trouble I've seen. Nobody knows but Jesus." He knows, He cares, and He carries.

When hardship and sorrow transport us to desert places we can take heart in the words of Deuteronomy 32:

"In a desert land he found him, in a barren and howling waste. He shielded him and cared for him; he guarded him as the apple of his eye, like an eagle that stirs up its nest and hovers over its young, that spreads its wings to catch them and carries them on its pinions" (verses 10-11).

God finds us in our barrenness. He guards us and hovers over us. When we free-fall, His wings are there to catch and carry us.[48]

The Lord longs to be gracious to us and rises to show us

compassion.[49] His love and mercy compel Him to rise and minister to us. What grace!

Grace is Our Only Certainty

Paul understood God's grace. The apostle suffered more than most of us. He was forcibly kicked out of cities and falsely accused. His tormentors stoned him and left him for dead. Soldiers stripped and beat him. He was wrongfully imprisoned, chained in stocks, and mercilessly whipped. Paul suffered from exposure, hunger, thirst, cold and nakedness. He endured three shipwrecks and lived in perpetual danger.[50] In all this, he did not expect defeat. He expected grace to triumph.

As a suffering servant, he testified, "Thanks be to God, who *always leads us in triumphant procession* in Christ."[51] Paul's expectation of grace was never disappointed. His attitude reflected that of the prophet Jeremiah.

Known as the weeping prophet, Jeremiah spent his life preaching to a people who rejected and tormented him. The Israelites refused to heed his prophetic warnings and ended up in Babylonian captivity. In the book of Lamentations (the title indicates the tone of the book), Jeremiah wrote chapters about the hardships that befell him and the Israelites. We feel his pain and identify with the words he penned in the middle of the book, "My splendor is gone and all that I had hoped from the Lord. I remember my affliction and my wandering, the bitterness and the gall. I well remember them, and my soul is downcast within me."[52]

Even though his life was filled with failure, persecution, and captivity, Jeremiah's words don't end here. After citing his loss, affliction, wandering, and the bitterness of life, he does not yield to hopelessness. He adds the word *yet*—

> "Yet…this I call to mind and therefore I have hope:
> Because of the Lord's great love we are not consumed,
> for his compassions never fail.
> They are new every morning; great is your faithfulness."[53]

Yet, however, but, despite all I've endured and all I've lost, I have hope—because of the Lord's great love. Jeremiah expected God's grace. He anticipated its arrival, fresh every morning. He wrote, "The Lord is good to those whose *hope* is in him, to the one who seeks him; it is good to *wait* quietly for the salvation of the Lord."[54]

Every morning we open our eyes to grace. It is ready for us the moment we need it—grace to carry us through, grace sufficient for every need, grace in every situation.

Great Expectations

The God of all hope invites us to reject negativity and the gloomy predictions of Murphy's laws. There's a higher law that governs our lives and offers great expectations.

"In all things God works for the good of those who love him, who have been called according to his purpose."[55] Expect good.

"And God is able to make all grace abound to you, so that in all things at all times, having all that you need, you will abound in every good work."[56] Expect supply.

"And the God of all grace, who called you to his eternal glory in

Christ, after you have suffered a little while, will himself restore you and make you strong, firm and steadfast."[57] Expect restoration.

"Let us then approach the throne of grace with confidence, so that we may receive mercy and find grace to help us in our time of need."[58] Expect grace—and receive hope.

---

[44] 1 Timothy 1:17

[45] Psalm 139:8-12

[46] Isaiah 43:2

[47] Isaiah 43:4

[48] Deuteronomy 31:6

[49] Isaiah 30:18a

[50] 2 Corinthians 11:23-27

[51] 2 Corinthians 2:14 (emphasis added)

[52] Lamentations 3:18-20

[53] Lamentations 3:22-23

[54] Lamentations 3:25-26 (emphasis mine)

[55] Romans 8:28

[56] 2 Corinthians 9:8

[57] 1 Peter 5:10-11

[58] Hebrews 4:16

For Personal Reflection

Points to Ponder

- Life is a pilgrimage—we're going *through*.
- Faith tells us that if something goes wrong, God is there, regardless of feelings or fears.
- To say God is invisible is to declare that He is present, but not seen.
- My feelings amid personal chaos mean nothing—God is there and, because He is present, I can expect grace.
- The old spiritual tells a timeless truth, "Nobody knows the trouble I've seen. Nobody knows but Jesus."

Thoughts to Journal

- Write out the E of Hope.
- What has blasted a hole in your life? Have you tried to fill it?
- Identify the specific fears that taunt you.
- Consider the situations where God seems invisible. Acknowledge that though unseen, He is present.
- Choose which of Jeremiah's confessions will be yours:
  - ~ "My splendor is gone and all that I had hoped from the Lord. I remember my affliction and my wandering, the bitterness and the gall. I well remember them, and my soul is downcast within me."

~ "Yet...this I call to mind and therefore I have hope: Because of the Lord's great love we are not consumed, for his compassions never fail. They are new every morning; great is your faithfulness."

♦ Are you willing to change your expectations?

CHAPTER 10

How the "E" of Hope Sustained Me

Stacey's preschool teacher said that my three-year-old was a bubble—a happy, bouncing, energetic bubble. I never forgot it because her description was spot-on, not only when Stacey was three but even when she was fifteen, twenty-three and thirty. No one lit up a room like Stacey.

We named her Stacey Joy because it means *renewal of joy*. We were denied a child the first time we applied for adoption due to our unexpected pregnancy, but when we reapplied, we were rewarded with Stacey. She renewed our joy. We did not realize the suitability of her name as a baby would find expression in many facets of her life.

Stacey's emotions lived near the surface, from infancy into adulthood. It always surprised me that as quickly as her tears came, so did her smiles. Stacey did not hold a grudge or harbor resentment. Her troubles gave way to hope with the smallest encouragement. She lived in a state of renewed joy and shared it with others. Her sensitivity brought compassion and support to those around her.

And Stacey laughed. She laughed with a joy that bubbled up inside and spilled out, engaging others. Her laughter was often heard before she was seen. Her practical joking was good-natured, never vindictive or sarcastic.

Any success was reason for a party and Stacey was the first one to call friends together to celebrate. Her signature congratulatory phrase was *You go, girl!* spoken sincerely and without a trace of envy. She knew what it was to rejoice with those who rejoice.

Our *Renewal of Joy* did what her name declared—she brought joy wherever she went. When Stacey died, a spark died in all of us.

It's hard to talk about the events involved in the unforeseen death of a child and harder yet to find words that describe the tumult of feelings. The pain was amazing, the sorrow debilitating. Though exhausted, I resisted sleep because I knew that waking would mean fresh pain. Like rousing from a dream that blurs reality, each morning I dealt with the agonizing reminder that, yes, Stacey really did die, and then I would work through the horror of that truth. Again and again.

I came to the place where I realized that I now lived with a hole in my life. This was my new normal. Life would never be the same and I would never be the same. The hole was a permanent part of me—forever mine. I didn't argue about it or rationalize it. I just knew it. But then a question arose that consumed me. What do I do with the hole?

For weeks that was my constant prayer. "Lord, what do I do with the hole?" The hole both frightened and mesmerized me. It was menacing, dark, vast. I would not go near its edge for fear of falling in and being swallowed up. I could get lost in there! It was a hideous hole and its presence preoccupied me.

I understood immediately that I could not fill it. Nothing would fill the void of that hole. I also knew that it wouldn't close like a wound that eventually heals leaving only a scar. If I couldn't fill it and it wouldn't close, what could I do with it? I became petrified of the hole. It was deep; it was threatening; it was unexplored.

I feared that the hole would consume me and that I would become the hole. I feared it would define me, that all my decisions and future days would be dictated by the hole. I feared I would be known by it. *See her? She's the woman with the hole.* These thoughts may not have been rational, but in my grief they were real and I grappled with them every day.

Even if I tried to ignore it, the hole would be there, gaping and pulsating in my heart. It would be easy to obsess over it and rehearse how it got there, wondering if I could have prevented it or assigning blame to others. That would make it the focus of my life, the very thing I feared. Definitely not the route I wanted to take.

The greatest threat was that I would live in the hole, in the place of what-ifs and what could have been. Bound by the walls of the hole, it would become my life. I could hear myself saying, "Hello. My name is Barbara. Do you want to hear about my hole?" There had to be a way to live with a hole, but I didn't know how. It was dark; it was threatening; it was unknown. I couldn't see the bottom.

I began to take a practical approach. How would I deal with a hole in the ground? I listed my options. I could cover the hole with something, maybe a layer of sod or a piece of plywood. But that would increase the danger—what if the cover wore thin or blew off or caved in? I could unwittingly step on it and fall into the hole. At least if it was obvious I would be cautious.

Maybe I could put a fence around it. Could it be fenced in? There would always be a memory, an event, a fragrance, a song to yank the posts from the ground and collapse the fence, leaving the hole exposed.

I considered beautifying it. I could plant flowers and shrubs around it, maybe put a birdbath next to it. But this might give me a false security. If I pretended there was no danger, the façade of beauty could lure me close enough to slip into its bottomless abyss. I was frustrated.

My daughter, my friend, my cheerleader, my bubble was gone. *Lord, what do I do with the hole?* Day after day I asked this question until one day, God answered me. I was home, going about my affairs, when He spoke to my heart with its recently formed hole. In a whisper of grace He simply said, "You make of it a well."

A well! A well is a good thing. The hole is no longer negative but positive. A hole is empty, a well is full. A hole threatens, a well refreshes. A hole represents loss, damage, need. A well speaks of supply, life, hope. A well goes deep and offers nourishment—for ourselves and for others. Yes, I would make my hole a well.

But how?

I needed to understand what is in the well—what does well-water represent? I had one more question for God and He had one more answer for me, as astounding as it was simple—the well holds grace. Grace for today's sorrow and tomorrow's fears. Grace for my hurting heart and aloneness. Grace to share with others. Grace to share my story with you.

I've learned to live with my hole but it no longer frightens me. Fear has turned to hope, dread to anticipation. Now I approach my hole with confidence and I always find grace to help in my time of need.[59] My well has not run dry and I have come to expect grace.

One day I decided to name my well, like the patriarchs did in days of old. I named it *Renewal of Joy*.

---

[59] Hebrews 4:16

For Personal Reflection

Points to Ponder

- Life would never be the same and I would never be the same. The hole was a permanent part of me forever.
- A hole is empty, a well is full. A hole threatens, a well refreshes.
- The well holds grace—grace for today's sorrow and tomorrow's fears. Grace for my hurting heart and aloneness. Grace to share with others.

Thoughts to Journal

- Does your hole scare you? Have you considered what you can do with it?
- A debit column lists losses; an asset column abounds with grace. You will live out of one or the other. What is your choice?
- Become a grace-giver. The more we give, the greater our supply. Grace doesn't decrease with giving—it increases.

—E—

Living a Hope-<u>FUL</u> Life

The principles I offer in this book work. I've tested them and continue to prove them true. The moment I detect hopelessness edging its way into my heart I question myself in the four areas of H-O-P-E.

> H — Am I failing to recognize that there's a higher purpose than what I see? Am I mindful that God's thoughts are greater than I understand?
>
> O — Am I open to other possibilities? Is fear or comfort boxing me in?
>
> P — What is my thought pattern? If negative thoughts are my default, what positives can replace them?
>
> E — Do I expect grace? Or have I lost sight of my Heavenly Father's love?

Consistently choosing to walk these paths of H-O-P-E will renew our hope. They will allow us to live with optimism, not pessimism;

with anticipation, not dread; with confidence, not fear; with peace, not panic; with expectation, not despair. Exercising these options will invigorate our hope, but to live a hope*ful* lifestyle we need tenacity.

Hope-**F**UL

Hopeful people are willing to *fight* for what is theirs—fullness of life,[60] joy,[61] the freedom to live and serve.[62] Although our natural desire is for rest, not battle, hopeful people will not surrender to despair. Yielding to the enemy's temptation to give up is not an option. We refuse to be rendered ineffective.

Confidence to fight comes from selah-ing the Word of God. It strengthens our resolve and gives us the tenacity to endure under the weight of our burdens. In the face of despair we are able to grit our teeth and proclaim with certainty that all things will work together for our blessing because we love God.[63] That kind of resolve comes when the Word is settled in our hearts.

Belonging to God makes us many things—sheep, light, salt, servants, heirs, His children. It also makes us soldiers.[64] We are enlisted by the greatest King to do warfare for the greatest kingdom. Don't buckle under assault. Fight for hope. Christ secured it for us, we must not surrender it.

Hope-F**U**L

Hopeful people *understand* life from an eternal perspective. They recognize that, though painful, life's hardships are temporary, not permanent. The realization that our challenges are short-term makes it easier to endure. We submit to surgery knowing we will feel better. We work long hours knowing the paycheck will provide for our family. We endure sleepless nights and countless diaper changes knowing the baby will grow up. We persevere in trials because we know the reward awaiting us far outweighs the troubles we face.[65] There is more to life than our years on earth.

Jesus told His disciples they were facing difficult days. He offers us the same assurance He offered them, "In this world you will have trouble. But take heart! I have overcome the world."[66] He has overcome and faith in Him makes us overcomers. Our pain is temporal—our joy is eternal.

God has already seated us in heavenly places. We await the day when His incomparable riches will be ours, endlessly.[67] So what is a year, or five years, or ten years, in the light of our forever existence? Let's live on earth with heaven in mind, understanding the brevity of life and savoring the joy of a future without tears or fears, a future that will satisfy every longing and delight our hearts with undreamed pleasures.

Hope-FUL

Hopeful people *live*. Jesus said He came that we "may have life and have it to the full."[68] The Greek word He used for life is *zoe*, which means the absolute fullness of life, vitality. Zoe life is a life of hope.

Before we were born, He prepared our days and specific work for us to do.[69] We have purpose, value, and destiny because God wove it into our DNA when He created our inmost being and knit us together in our mother's womb. He saw us before we were formed and beholds us as we are now.[70] God has a reason for us to be alive today. He has things for us to do. Our days, and the opportunities they hold, are gifts to cherish.

Hopeful people count their blessings. They are content with who they are and the tasks before them. Even in the midst of failure, they resist negative thoughts and determine to trust God. Their choice is to live and bless others in the process.

Be Blessed

The day is coming when the sun of righteousness will rise with healing in its wings.[71] We will be free of earth's pain—no more aching, limping, wounds, abrasions, or tender spots. Hope's enemies will be vanquished and we will leap like calves released from the stall—free, vibrant and unrestrained.[72] As we wait for that day, we press forward and embrace hope.

Hold your eyes higher. Open your heart. Ponder the positive. Expect grace. Despair will flee and hope will swell your heart and overflow.

"May the God of hope fill you with all joy and peace as you trust in him, so that you may overflow with hope by the power of the Holy Spirit."[73]

---

60 John 10:10

61 John 15:11

62 John 8:36, Romans 6:18

63 Romans 8:28

64 2 Timothy 2:3-4

65 2 Corinthians 4:17

66 John 16:33

67 Ephesians 2:6-7

68 John 10:10

69 Psalm 139:16, Ephesians 2:10

70 Psalm 34:15, Jeremiah 32:19

71 Malachi 4:2a

72 Malachi 4:2b

73 Romans 15:13

For Personal Reflection

Points to Ponder

- Hopeful people are willing to *fight* for what is theirs—they don't buckle under assault.
- Hopeful people *understand* life from an eternal perspective.
- Hopeful people *live* and bless others in the process.
- Hold your eyes higher. Open your heart. Ponder the positive. Expect grace.

Thoughts to Journal

- Are you willing to fight for hope? How can you put more of God's Word in your heart?
- What thought patterns do you need to change to better understand life from God's perspective?
- Choose life. Begin by listing ten blessings and make it a daily habit.

A H-O-P-E Assessment

H Hold your eyes Higher
Where are my eyes looking? What situation am I focused on today?

_____

_____

_____

_____

Lord, I hold my eyes above what I see and acknowledge your higher plans and purposes.

_____

_____

_____

_____

O Open your eyes to God's Opportunities
What status quo plans am I clinging to? What desires do I need to release?

_____

_____

_____

_____

Lord, I will forget the former things and not dwell on the past (Isaiah 43:18). Open my eyes to see the new thing you are doing. This is my prayer of relinquishment:

_____

_____

_____

_____

P Ponder the Positive, not the Problems
What problem am I rehashing? Have my thoughts changed anything?

_____

_____

_____

_____

Lord, I confess I've been pondering my problems, a lot. Though they are real, I will ponder the higher truth of your Word, with the Holy Spirit to help and remind me.

_____

_____

_____

_____

E Expect Grace
What am I afraid of? What negative expectations do I need to relinquish?

_____
_____
_____
_____

Lord, I will expect grace. I base my expectation on this verse about your grace and love:

_____
_____
_____
_____

While in the process of publishing this book, I waded through deep waters of pain and challenge. Tears flowed for two days and despair threatened before I, your humble author, remembered to evaluate my H-O-P-E levels. I created this assessment from that place of need. I hope you find it useful.

> "And the God of all grace, who called you to his eternal
> glory in Christ, after you have suffered a little while, will
> himself restore you and make you strong, firm
> and steadfast."
> 1 PETER 5:10-11

Dear Reader,

I wrote this book for you, my fellow traveler on the road of suffering. So many times I wanted to quit writing and hide my pain from unknown eyes, but you urged me on. The belief that my journey could help someone who is broken propelled me. This book is my arm around your shoulder.

I pray these four paths of hope will enable you to better trust the God who sees all and loves you deeply. May your brokenness find healing and hope fill your heart anew.

I would love to hear your story and, while I can't answer all letters, I will pray for you. You can reach me at bhigby9323@gmail.com and visit my website at barbarahigbyhope.com.

For God is my witness, how I yearn for you all with the affection of Christ Jesus. Philippians 1:8 ESV

CPSIA information can be obtained
at www.ICGtesting.com
Printed in the USA
LVHW091931110619
620921LV00001B/1/P